No-Nonsense Networking

The Straightforward Guide to Making Productive, Profitable and Prosperous Contacts and Connections

Timothy M. Houston

www.tmhouston.com

Houston-CB Group, Inc., publisher

ISBN-13: 978-0692740941

The Legal Stuff

DEDICATED TO YOU:

THE READER AND TO MY FRIENDS,
FAMILY, STUDENTS, CLIENTS, AND FANS

---

*I write this not for
the many, but for
you; each of us is
enough of an
audience for the
other.*

—Epicurus

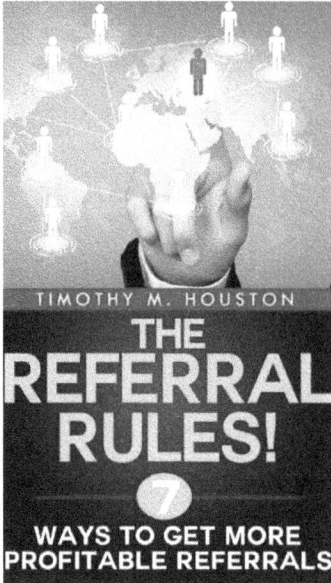

TABLE OF CONTENTS

What is Networking And Why This Book? ....- 1 -

Chapter 1: Preparing to Network ....- 7 -

Your Pre-Networking Checklist ....- 8 -

    Item #1: Ask yourself 3 Important Questions ....- 10 -

    Item #2: 4 Questions Always Asked by Effective
    Networkers ....- 13 -

    Item #3: Online Observations and Social Media
    Surveillance ....- 16 -

    Item #4: Does Your Image Match Your Message? .....- 21 -

    Item #5: Set Your Watch to Lombardi Time ....- 25 -

    Item #6: Get Your Wingmen in Formation ....- 29 -

Chapter 2: Ready? Set? Network! ....- 33 -

How to Talk To Strangers ....- 34 -

    Should I Start Off With Small Talk? ....- 35 -

    NSFN: Avoiding The Taboo Topics ....- 38 -

    The Answer to the Dreaded Question! ....- 42 -

    Introducing the Intriguing Introduction: ....- 43 -

    Ditch the Pitch: ....- 47 -

So What Do You *REALLY* TALK About? ....- 49 -

    Focus on Their Favorite Subject ....- 51 -

    The #1 Skill of Master Conversationalists ....- 53 -

    The One Powerful Question That is Rarely Asked .....- 53 -

To Give or Not To Give Your Business Card ....- 55 -

How to End and Exit With Ease ....- 60 -

Concluding the Conversation...........................- 60 -

Beware the Networking Ghosts....................- 62 -

Ethical Endings and Exits by Susan RoAne............- 68 -

Chapter 3: After Networking Know-Hows ....- 73 -

The Fortune is in The Follow-Through And The Follow-Up ...- 74 -

Tim's 3-Step Follow-Through System ....- 76 -

How About Now? ....- 78 -

Flawless Follow-Up in 4 Steps ....- 78 -

The One Thing… ....- 82 -

How to Meet People You Didn't Meet ....- 84 -

Your Next Steps ....- 87 -

Before You Go…....................................- 88 -

Meet Tim Houston....................................- 89 -

Download Your FREE COPY! ....- 91 -

Endnotes..- 93 -

WHAT IS NETWORKING AND WHY THIS BOOK?

"Everyone's connected, but no one is connecting. The human element has long been missing. Tell me, have you seen it? Have you seen it?"

— Armin Van Buuren,
"Alone"

If you ask ten random people how they would define the word "networking," you would probably receive ten different answers, in two different tones. Some people will answer in a positive manner because they see it as a worthwhile activity that can produce very positive results both in the short and long-term.

But others will respond very negatively. They see networking as a manipulative process which seeks to promote a personal agenda and priorities. They also view networking as a "numbers game", as if it was all about how many people can they meet at one event. Too often they also equate networking with selling – something that it is not.

In my book, ***The World's Worst Networker***, I defined networking as follows:

> "The creation of new relationships and the enhancement of existing ones through a process of engagement for the purpose of mutual personal and business development."

You are probably thinking to yourself: "That definition sounds a bit academic as if it were from a textbook or a college course on marketing."

So to put it another way, networking is all about three simple steps:

1. You are willing to meet new people and also deepen existing relationships with those that you know.
2. You are willing to build an authentic, honest relationship with them. (This is the step that is not followed by those people who are the really bad networkers. It is also the main reason why the process of networking is given a bad name).

3. It is all about finding ways to help others without immediately expecting anything in return for ourselves.

Networking is not a part-time or occasional exercise. Everywhere we go, we have the opportunity to network with others. The dilemma that most people face is how to do it in an effective, comfortable manner.

You probably bought this book because you want to be a better networker. Maybe you are just starting out in your career or got a new job. Perhaps you moved into a new field and need to develop and build contacts. Maybe you are already established in your business but need more visibility so that people know more about your services or products. Perhaps you go to networking events and feel that they are a waste of time and money because you meet and talk to the "wrong people". Maybe you find the entire networking process and experience to be very daunting.

Whatever your reason, you're about to get the help and guidance you want and need.

So what makes this book different from the dozens of that offer advice on "how to network?"

First, because *No-Nonsense Networking* is a straight-to-the-point primer/reminder about the fundamentals of networking, it is a short read which is intentional and by design. As you read through the book, I am going to provide you with efficient, effective and powerful methods and techniques that you can use in your networking efforts. I don't want you to spend hours reading; instead, my goal is to take what you learn and put it into practice. I would suggest that you first read it from cover to cover and then go back to focus on a particular subject, strategy or technique that you want to learn and /or refine.

Second, as your teacher and guide, my job is to make things understandable and simple. Unfortunately, it has become commonplace for many authors of business books to put together examples and anecdotes and then try to build a "theory" around it, hoping that it works. It is also to no one's benefit if I were to teach you some convoluted, impractical techniques and strategies, full of "corporate speak" that may look impressive as part of the thesis for an MBA degree but ultimately fails or is impractical in the real world. Likewise, there are many other books and programs that are just too complicated and take too much time to implement.

Each topic and technique in this book is taught in a very direct and to the point manner and is based on actual experience and consistent results.

You can expect there to be no fluff, no untried theories and definitely no-nonsense in what is taught. In a very a straightforward, "down and dirty" manner, by the end of this book, you will know:

- What to do before, during and after attending a networking event so that you can derive the most benefit from the experience.
- How to implement easy, non-threatening, authentic step-by-step techniques that will help you to meet people and make new contacts.
- How to refine and master the art of networking so that you can enter the next stage which will focus on deepening the relationship in order to transform these new contacts into quality connections.

Let's start making your networking efforts more productive, profitable and prosperous!

CHAPTER 1:

PREPARING TO NETWORK

Your Pre-Networking Checklist

"Success depends on previous preparation and without such preparation there is sure to be failure."

– Confucius

I attend hundreds of networking events each year, ranging from multi-day conferences and conventions to weekly referral group meetings. Quite often I find that some of the people attending these events are not fully prepared to network with others. Some lack pens and business cards. Others don't know what to say when they meet someone.

While I wish to say I'm surprised to experience this, I'm not. After 20+ years as a business owner who lives and does business "in the trenches and not in the Ivory Tower," I have come to appreciate and know what works well when it comes to business networking and what doesn't.[1]

---

[1] My first book, ***The World's Worst Networker*** focused on the true stories and in some cases the true confessions of the

Showing up to a networking event unprepared or with little care clearly doesn't work well at all. Even worse, being unprepared or unwilling to do the post networking activities required makes your networking efforts a complete waste of time, energy, and money for everyone involved.

One of the first lessons learned by every aircraft pilot at flight school is that they must have a written pre-flight checklist to be used to conduct an inspection of the aircraft. It is a standard procedure that starts even before they enter into the aircraft and is conducted in a specific step-by-step pattern. Similarly, you need to have a pre-networking checklist in place which consists of adequate preparation, research, and planning. Doing so will make your networking more effective, fun and less nerve wracking.

What follows is the outline and explanation of my pre-networking checklist consisting of just 6 items.

"nightmares of networking": the people that give the process such a tarnished reputation

ITEM #1: ASK YOURSELF 3 IMPORTANT QUESTIONS

To best prepare for any networking situation, you need to ask yourself these three basic, but incredibly important questions.

Question #1: "What is my *reason* for attending the networking event?"

Basically, ask yourself why do you want to go? For example, a survey was conducted of 4,449 business people from around the world by BNI, the world's largest business referral, and networking organization. They were asked the question: "What is your primary reason for networking?" 78.5% of the respondents indicated "new business" as their number one reason for networking, 12.7% said "career advancement" and just 6.7% said "education" [i]. Having a clear enough reason to network will help you to make good use of your time and others'.

(Please don't confuse your reason with your goal as these are very different yet often confused activities. Dictionary.com defines "reason" as "the basis or cause, as for some belief, action, fact, event, etc."[ii] "Goal" is defined as "the result or achievement toward which effort is directed; aim, end.") [iii]

Question #2: "What *goal* do I want to achieve by attending the event?"

Mark Victor Hansen, co-author of the *Chicken Soup for the Soul* series says *"Networking without a goal is an exercise in going nowhere, fast."* The second step is to determine and commit to setting your networking goals.

Your goal may be to ultimately find potential clients through referrals. It could be to meet people who may be able to introduce you to others who you can help, and who can also help you. It may be to expand your current network of trusted business advisors and partners; it may be to get a new job. Whatever the goal is, it must be clearly defined *before* you start networking so that you can direct your networking efforts towards achieving that particular goal.

Question #3: Does the event justify my costs in terms of time, energy and money?

There are just some events that are not worth going to. The people attending may not be the people you need or want to meet if they are outside of your field or target market. The type of the event may also not be best suited for you.

It may not be the right time for you to attend. For example, you may need to focus your efforts, time, energy—and to a degree, money – on deepening relationships with those you have already met *instead* of meeting new people. There may be other things to attend to in your business that take priority over networking.

You need to be a bit discriminating in your selection of the networking events you want to attend. Do not react by accepting every invitation that is offered to you.

ITEM #2: 4 QUESTIONS ALWAYS ASKED BY EFFECTIVE NETWORKERS

So you have determined your reason, set a goal and made a decision to attend a particular networking event. There is still some preparation that is needed before you arrive. You need to contact and ask the following questions of the **organizer of the event.**

Question #1: "Who are the expected attendees?"

Are they entrepreneurs who own multiple businesses? Will there be many employees of a particular company represented? Are directors of non-profit organizations scheduled to attend? By knowing the types of people who are expected to attend the event, you will be best-prepared to know "how" to network with them.

Question #2: "What is the format of the event?"

Networking events typically follow two types of formats: **open networking** and **structured**. It is important that you know the format ahead of time so that you are best prepared, especially if you are expected to speak at these events.

Open networking events typically have very little structure. Attendees are expected to move around and meet others on their own. Many business card exchanges and/or cocktail hours follow this format. There may be some brief remarks made by the organizer and sponsors but aside from thanking the attendees for coming and some promotional activities or announcements, people are free to come and go as they please.

Structured/Formal networking events are different. Networking groups and service organizations (Rotary, Kiwanis, etc.) usually have an agenda or format that is followed at their meetings. Members of these organizations usually have an opportunity to speak in turn, and then guests are invited to introduce themselves. There are usually set time-limits for things to take place at these types of events. (i.e. a defined start and end time, a limit on the amount of time allocated to specific discussions and presentations, etc.)

Some events may be a combination of open networking and structured. Many years ago, I attended a Chamber of Commerce monthly business after-hours mixer where they gave new chamber members and visitors in attendance a 1-minute opportunity to introduce themselves to the crowd. After the introductions, everyone was left to mix, meet and mingle on their own.

Question #3: "What is the dress code?"

While most business people will assume that formal business attire is appropriate for networking events that may not always the case. Depending on where you live, sometimes the local culture and customs dictate the dress code. For example, while in Aruba, I attended a networking event that was held at a restaurant that was on a beach and the dress code was very "smart casual." I went to another event outside of Dallas, Texas at a ranch where wearing jeans, cowboy boots and hats were perfectly acceptable among those wearing business attire.

On social networking sites like Meetup.com, you can find everything from groups developed around special interests and themes that hold regular get-togethers and networking events. Often these gatherings are held in more casual settings. Sometimes conferences and multi-day, large gatherings will have additional and optional activities ranging from pub crawls to going to a concert or baseball game with other attendees. You always want to make sure you have dressed appropriately for the occasion.

Question #4: "Can an attendee list be made available before or after the event?"

Some events like conferences and seminars will supply a list of attendees, sometimes with their contact information like an email address or phone number. Meetup.com and Facebook groups often show the names and profiles of those who RSVPed to attend an event and even allow them the write a message or other introduction which is shown on the registration page. But not every organization will provide an attendee list. If you are attending an event and are able to secure a copy of the attendee list, you will be holding a potential goldmine of information and potential relationships. (You will learn an incredible technique and strategy later in this book that will utilize attendee lists in an ethical manner).

ITEM #3: ONLINE OBSERVATIONS AND SOCIAL MEDIA SURVEILLANCE

Once you have decided on a networking event asked and received answers to your questions from the organizers, there's still a bit of preparation to do before you actually attend. You now need to do some online observations and social media surveillance of the potential attendees.

Online Observations

When you are invited to attend an event do some research on the hosts and sponsors. Who are they? How often do they conduct these types of events? Some organizations hold just one big conference or networking event each a year while others have weekly or monthly activities ranging from meetings to mixers. Not only should you review the hosts' corporate or official websites, if they have a dedicated website for the event you are considering attending, take note of it. Look for the following:

- If there are workshops or break-out sessions that may be conducted as part of the bigger event, determine who the facilitators are and research them on sites like LinkedIn.

- If there is a keynote speaker, take note of who they are and what their topics will be. Do some research about the speaker and come prepared to ask a question during the event (if allowed) or if you're given the opportunity to meet them after their speech. (If you do have the opportunity to speak with them, please do not monopolize all their time! Ask your question, ask for an autograph and/or a selfie and then move on.)

- Several events feature panel discussions with experts and authorities about a given subject. Find out the focus of the panel and do some research into each of the panelists. These panel discussions often offer audience members the opportunity to ask questions. You will be surprised at how often other audience members and sometimes even members of the panel will actually seek out or interact with the person who asks a great question after the panel discussion is over.

- Some multi-day events such as conferences and seminars have information about the specific individuals who are in charge of coordinating and producing the event. Take note as to who they are as well as any interesting information about them that is listed on the event's page as you will be using this information in your post-networking activities, explained in Chapter 3.

- Some organizers will use online ticket/registration services like EventBrite.com as they give the option of showing their attendees in real-time. If available, I will often look at the list several times before the event to see if I know anyone who is attending or if there are particular people who I would want to meet at the event. Smaller events use sites like MeetUp.com where attendee information and profiles are often shown to those who register to attend.

- Does the website allow you to receive updates about the event? If so, opt-in to receive them so that you have the latest information about any additions or changes to the program.

Social Media Surveillance

You should also follow the organizer or organization on social media sites like Twitter, LinkedIn, Pinterest, Instagram, and Facebook. Many of them will create a special event page on Facebook and/or LinkedIn, post promotional pictures on Pinterest and Instagram or they may use a special hashtag on Instagram or Twitter. The people who are attending the event may link, share, retweet and reference the event page. You may want to meet or communicate with these people before going.

Once you register to attend, some events will even allow you to link your social media accounts to their page so that you can see which of your friends/connections/followers are also going and/or allow you to share the fact that you registered to attend with the people in your social networks. While this is more of an advertising strategy from the organizer's perspective, it can be a gold mine of information for you.

If you see that people you know are attending, you can contact them to let them know that you will be in attendance as well. Also, for people you don't know well enough but who you want to meet, you could also see if they are connected to any of your connections/friends/followers. If they are, ask your friend how well they know them and would they be willing to introduce you to them at or ahead of the event. Offer to return the favor for the people they would like to meet.

Because of their nature, social networking sites like Facebook could reveal life changes such as when someone got married or had a child or if it was or will be someone's birthday. Sites like LinkedIn will tell you the person's professional history such as where they worked what other organizations (professional and social) they belong to.

Gathering this information through Social Media Surveillance can be very useful and valuable while you are networking as, when used properly and discerningly, it could leave a positive or memorable impression with others because you took the time to do your research.

ITEM #4: DOES YOUR IMAGE MATCH YOUR MESSAGE?

"The perception of images is the reality of our contemporary culture."

—Madonna

We were taught by our parents that we should not prejudge; that looks alone are not important. While this advice has good intentions, when it comes to marketing, advertising, and even networking it is ***all about your image***. How you project yourself to a potential customer and networking partners is vital.

When two people meet for the first time, they immediately form initial ideas about each other. These early impressions have a major impact on how their relation further develops. People's behavior towards others is shaped depending on differences in first impressions such that people who have favorable impressions of someone tend to interact **more** with that person than others having unfavorable impressions. First impressions are, therefore, an important basis for whether humans will build rich relations with others.[iv]

When you are networking, you are doing more than just marketing your business; you are actually marketing yourself. Most people will develop an impression of you within the first seven seconds of meeting you. This impression will become undeniably fixed in their mind as it will extend beyond you and goes on to include to your business, the people you associate with and the people you hire or work with.

Your message is not just what you say and how you say it, but how you appear to them both physically in person as well as online. Evidence from social psychology has demonstrated that initial impressions are formed rather quickly on the basis of minimal information with visual appearance and nonverbal behavior providing the major cues.[v]

It seems that at most networking events that I attend, there will be at least one person at each event whose image does not match their message.

For example, at one networking event, I met a business attorney named Sam who had worked for almost 10 years in a prestigious law firm. While at the firm, he represented several well-known, worldwide companies, and also many local companies. His knowledge of the law was what one would expect of a seasoned attorney. The firm was first-rate and everyone who worked there looked, and acted, first-rate: from the most senior partner to the people working in the mail-room.

Six months prior to our meeting, Sam had left the firm and opened his own private practice. He joined a local networking group to build his practice and was accepted. However, after a few months, he began to complain that he did not get any referrals.

When I visited his group I noticed that he showed up to the meetings in a t-shirt and sweatpants, unshaven and looking like he just rolled out of bed. I later found out from his fellow members that this was not an isolated incident – he showed up almost every week, unkempt.

Members who visited his office found it very sloppy and messy. When some people tried to approach him about appearing more organized and professional, he was taken aback by their comments. He would reply by telling them how he spent 80+ hours a week in a suit and tie for almost a decade while at the firm and since he was his own boss now, he could do whatever he wanted.

Several members secretly confided in me that they could not refer clients to him because of his public image. These potential referral givers felt that even though Sam may have known his stuff, he reflected poorly on *them* due to his public image which did not match his professional message.

On the other hand, you don't want to wear something outrageous either. Whenever attending a networking meeting, a business dinner, or meeting a new or current client, it is important to remember that their spotlight is focused on you. Make sure that you are "dressed for work". If you are a landscaper, a polo shirt with your business' name on it is appropriate, on the other hand, if you are a CPA or an attorney, men, a suit and tie are expected and women, a business suit or conservative dress is expected. (Consult the Pre-Networking Checklist Item #2, Question #3).

Your business' image helps to build people's trust, confidence, and the motivation to do business with and refer business to you. You want them to remember **YOU**, not your clothes (except, of course, if you are a fashion designer or model). Make sure that you look the part. Simply put, the more professional you are, look and behave, the better the first impression will be with the people that you meet for the first time, as well as with those you will meet again and again.

ITEM #5: SET YOUR WATCH TO LOMBARDI TIME

"People count the faults of those who keep them waiting"

-- French Proverb

Attending a networking event means more than just showing up. It means showing up on time or ahead of time whenever we are meeting with people who are or may become clients, networking partners or referral sources.

You need to treat each event you attend and each person you are meeting as if it were a business appointment with one of your best clients – even if you are just meeting these people for the very first time.

The famous football coach, Vince Lombardi developed a principle which is referred to as "Lombardi Time" which means that one should show up to wherever they are going 15 minutes early, or else be considered late. Whenever rookie football players on the Fordham Rams and later, the Green Bay Packers and journalists covering a game didn't show up at least 15 minutes prior to a bus or plane's scheduled departure for a road-game, or for a scheduled practice, they would find themselves out in the cold –- literally!

Using Lombardi time is extremely important when going to business meetings or networking events as it will provide you with the extra time to catch your breath, get prepared and focus on the tasks that you're about to undertake. It also provides extra time to spend interacting with others and gives you the advantage of meeting and introducing yourself to more new people

It is amazing to me that there are people who are consistently late or who consistently fail to show up for a meeting or an event, even if they promised to. While it may be acceptable to show up "fashionably late" to a social event, when it comes to networking and business events, showing up late can cost you a bundle in terms of your reputation and in potential business.

If you keep Lombardi Time, you have an advantage over those who don't in that you have the opportunity to observe the behavior of others. Are they frantically arriving at the meeting or are they strolling in without a care in the world, almost with pride of being late? (It makes you wonder if they conduct business the same way and can have a big impact on their reliability and ultimately, referability).

NEVER BE LATE AGAIN!

To keep Lombardi time, set your alarm clock, your watch/smartphone clock and the clock in your car 15 minutes ahead of the real time.

As you begin to become accustomed to this "new time", you will always arrive "on time" by being ahead of time.

ITEM #6: GET YOUR WINGMEN IN FORMATION

Networking is similar to dating in some respects. Sometimes we are comfortable and ready to approach people on our own but there are other times when we may need some additional help, especially with strangers or those who we are barely acquainted with. To make it easier, you sometimes need to have Wingmen with you at a networking event.

Wikipedia provides a great definition of the social aspect of a Wingman:

> "The Wingman is a role that a person may take when a friend needs support with approaching potential partners. A wingman is someone who is on the 'inside' and is used to help someone with relationships."[vi]

Having a networking Wingman/Wingwoman or two is an excellent technique to use because numerous research studies have uncovered that individual people, when situated within a group, tend to be perceived by others as more attractive and approachable than those who are alone. It is referred to as the *Cheerleader Effect.*

Citing several studies, Cindi May, Professor of Psychology at the College of Charleston explains in *Scientific American:*

"One of the components of the *Cheerleader Effect* is that the impression that we have of the group as a whole influences our perception of any one individual item. We tend to view individual members as being more like the group than they actually are. Thus when we see a face in a crowd, we tend to perceive that face as similar to the average of all the faces in that crowd[vii].

While networking here are three things you want to do with and for your Wingmen/Wingwomen:

1. Find out if they a) know any of the people you would like to meet that are attending the event and b) how well they know them.
2. Ask them if they would be willing to provide you with an enthusiastic introduction to those people.

3. Then ask them who *they* want to be introduced to and offer to return the favor with the same zeal and enthusiasm when introducing them.

At the end of the event remember to give and get some feedback from your Wingman/Wingwoman. Share your stories about the people you met, how you felt while meeting them with your Wingman/Wingwoman (i.e. were you nervous, relieved, grateful, etc) and finally your initial impressions and the prognosis for following up with them your new contacts after the event.

Patricia Fripp, CSP, CPAE is an executive speech coach and sales presentation skill trainer. She shares a networking technique she calls "Having your Own Public Relations Agent". She suggests that your partner(s) rehearse in advance how you will introduce each other. Here's a short, powerful video that illustrates the point: **https://youtu.be/SjiCy-wXoQg**

Chapter 2:

Ready? Set? Network!

HOW TO TALK TO STRANGERS

---

*"You can't stay in your corner
of the forest, waiting for
others to come to you; you
have to go to them
sometimes."*

-- Winnie the Pooh

You have arrived at the networking event and the inevitable happens:

Either someone approaches you or you have approached someone.

Now, you have to *say something!*

At this point, most people really don't know what to say. Ordinarily, most people will start by walking up to someone and introducing themselves by extending their hand and saying "My name is…." and the other person will often reply in kind.

Now an important, split-second decision needs to be made:

SHOULD I START OFF WITH SMALL TALK?

There are two schools of thought when it comes to small talk. There are those who believe that you should make small talk as it is essential to getting the conversation going; and then there are those who hate the whole idea of small talk, believing that it is inauthentic and a waste of time.

My opinion is that small talk is incredibly important when building new relationships and is necessary to do when networking, provided that it is not small-minded or trivial and it should never be inauthentic. Small talk helps to provide a bridge from saying "hello" to the substantive part of the conversation.

Other proponents of small talk agree. In *Psychology Today,* F. Diane Barth, a psychotherapist, teacher and author says:

> "[M]aking small talk is not only an important social skill, but it can make those happy hours less painful, earn you extra points, and give you important information about some of the best ways to work with some of your colleagues, and maybe even with your boss. It will also make family events, weddings, and other social occasions a lot more

interesting—and open doors to new friendships, new opportunities, or even a new relationship."[viii]

In her book, *What do I Say Next?*, author and speaker, Susan RoAne says:

"Small talk is the biggest talk we do…small talk is how we exchange information, preferences, ideas and opinions on issues. It's how we break the ice and get a sense of what people are, what they like and what they *are* like…Small talk is what we do to build the big talk. It is the schmoozing that cements relationship and success."[ix]

The Times of India quoted William Foley, professor of Linguistics at the University Sydney as saying:

"Small talk functions as a low-threat way to make connections with people. It's about elegantly starting, sustaining, and ending a dialogue with strangers or acquaintances."[x]

Gretchen Rubin, author of the *New York Times* #1 Bestseller, *The Happiness Project* created a helpful "Menu of Options for Making Small Talk" on her blog. Regardless if you are an introvert or an extrovert, these tips will come in very handy at your next networking event. See the list here: **http://bit.ly/smalltalkmenu**

NSFN: Avoiding The Taboo Topics

Certain videos, pictures and stories on the internet are deemed NSFW (Not Safe For Work) because they may be suggestive, lewd, crude or are an inappropriate topic that has no place in the workplace. There are similar "taboo topics" which are NSFN (Not Safe for Networking) and you should avoid talking about at all costs as they will undoubtedly cause people to become uneasy and in some cases combative with you. The taboo topics are:

1. Politics and Religion
2. Your Personal Life
3. Crude Jokes/Humor
4. Trash-Talking the competition.

Politics and Religion: Even though almost everyone will have an opinion about politics unless you are at a political convention or meeting, the topic is best left alone. The same is true about your religious beliefs. Dr. Ivan Misner, founder and Chief Visionary Officer of BNI, the world's largest business networking, and referral organization says: "Your politics simply aren't relevant to your professional life and your goal of building your business. A political discussion in the context of networking is distracting, and even worse, it can be divisive and detrimental to team building. If you want to stay on point about your business mission, stay off the topics of religion and politics in networking and other work-related meetings."[xi]

Your Personal Life: Whether it is about their dating life or complaining about their boss or talking about their kids or bragging about their own personal achievements, some people are all too eager and comfortable to talk about their personal life with complete strangers that they just met. Nor is the networking event is not an opportunity for you to pry into the personal lives of others. (Never ask "Are you single?" "What's your net worth?") There's a way to remain personal with others and still be professional. If something is going wrong at in your life please leave your "baggage" by the entrance to the room – it will be there on the way out. There's no need to bring it into the networking experience and burden others with it.

Crude Jokes/Humor: The late American humorist and author, Erma Bombeck once said: "There's a thin line that separates laughter and pain, comedy and tragedy, humor and hurt". The problem is that you don't know where that "thin line" is with most people. In this overly politically correct day and age, what one person finds hilarious another finds utterly offensive. Play it safe and stay away from any crude jokes or humor. You are not doing a stand-up routine at a comedy club and the people you are meeting did not come to hear jokes. You want to be remembered by others as a personable and professional and not the class clown.

Trash-Talking the Competition: Chances are at most networking events your competitors may be in the room. Even if they are not, you don't want to trash-talk your competitors when interacting with other people. Almost always, these backfires because the people you are talking to may end up believing that you are vindictive or jealous. Perhaps they may actually be using your competitor's products or services and *actually like them!* You also lose whatever rapport and trust you may have started to establish with the people you meet. (Ever think to yourself "I wonder what he/she says when I'm not around" after hearing someone say something bad about another person?)

When someone badmouths their competitors they are actually providing free publicity and creating ill-will towards each other. John Chapin, author of *The Sales*

Encyclopedia says: "When you start to badmouth the competition, you lower the perceived product value from your company as well as the competitors. It's akin to saying 'They're terrible. Obviously, we're not perfect because no one can be, yet we're not as bad as they are'. Bad mouthing the competition lowers the bar for everyone in your industry, including yours."[xii] Remember, word-of-mouth travels fast but negative word of mouth travels the fastest and reaches more people.

If someone asks you what the differences are between you and your competitors, point out the differences in a professional manner by accentuating the positives that you or your company offers.

THE ANSWER TO THE DREADED QUESTION!

"I suffer. What do you do?"

Shortly after you introduce yourself or after some small talk, the dreaded question is going to be asked: *"What do you do?"*

The usual response will be to state your profession. People's reactions may be mixed at this point. Some will want to talk to you while others may immediately make a judgment about you just because of an experience they had with someone in your profession, resulting in a very limited conversation. (In fact, according to a Gallup poll conducted from December 8-11, 2014, if you are a lawyer, business executive, ad agent, car salesperson or a member of the United States Congress, you are perceived as being the in the five most unethical and dishonest professions. If you are in one of the first four professions, don't despair: Members of Congress have only a 7% honest/ethical rating representing the worst perception of all professions).[xiii]

Your goal is to get them converse with you and to break through any judgment barriers they may have put up.

But how do you do it?

What if you could introduce yourself in a way that gets the other people interested in you, right from the outset of the conversation and builds trust and rapport?

Introducing the Intriguing Introduction:
Instead of just telling someone your name and title, you say something that is descriptive of what you do – not just your job but what you or what your products/services do for people, organizations or businesses – and is appealing to the listener. Think about your profession. What is it that you do? What benefits do you, your services/products offer to your target market?

For example, I will often introduce myself this way:

"Hello, I'm Tim Houston and I make businesses and business people more productive, profitable and prosperous."

Most of the time people will reply by asking me "How do you do that?" or "That's interesting, can you tell me more?"

Once they do that, it gives me permission to continue to talk a little bit more about myself in a way that is not boisterous but provides them with quality information.

If you are a payroll representative, instead of saying "My company offers payroll services," say "I help pay 8,000+ people each week, on time and without any delays."

If you sell disability insurance: "I make sure people are paid when they can't go to work due to an accident."

If you are in public relations: "I make people look great at 5 and 10 pm each day."

(You get the idea).

Another way to introduce yourself is to ask a thought-provoking question, make a statement or tell a fact and then to position yourself as the solution or answer to the question.

For example, a career coach may say "Did you know that Marketwatch reported that most employers are expected to give just a 3% raise to their employees in 2016[xiv] and Time Magazine recently reported that 70% of Americans hate their jobs?[xv] So instead of being miserable and underpaid, I help people to find fulfilling, financially rewarding careers, without settling for less"

A financial advisor may say "More than 43% of Americans are saving less than 5% of their annual income for emergencies and their retirement[xvi]. In fact, a Bankrate.com study found 1 in 3 Americans is near total financial disaster should they experience a severe, unexpected expense.[xvii] Well, I help people to financially protect themselves and to prepare for their retirement using the money they already make."

This type of introduction also works very well for those who are in professions that most people may have a hard time understanding what they really do.

For example, if you sold Search Engine Optimization (SEO) services, you could say: "You know how you type a word or phrase in Google and then a list of websites comes up? Well, I help businesses to be featured on page one, in the Top 10 results for their category or subject whenever someone does a search for what they offer."

A statement like this causes the person who is listening to you, to visualize themselves in their mind's eye actually searching on Google, seeing the results and looking for their name or their business' name on the first page.

Creating a strong Intriguing Introduction will not only cause the people you are interacting with to want to learn more about you, it will create a sense of rapport, trust, and goodwill, all of which are essential to successful networking.

"What you say to others is a reflection of who they think you are. While you are speaking they are thinking and deciding who you are, whether they like you, and whether they want to take the next step with you."

– Jeffrey Gitomer, The Little Black Book of Connections.

Ditch the Pitch:

After you introduce yourself, do not try to pitch your products and services to the people you meet while networking. When you are networking, you are not selling. No one goes to a networking event to actually buy something, so don't even try to sell your services to them.

Whenever I get "pitched" by someone I meet for the first time, I liken it to walking up to a complete stranger, saying hello and asking them if they want to get married and live with you for the rest of their life. To paraphrase Dale Carnegie, when networking you want to make friends and influence people, not create enemies and isolate yourself by burning a bridge you were trying to build towards a new relationship. Simply put, you are networking to build new relationships, not close a deal.

> Bestselling author and speaker, Bob Burg offers some wise advice on this topic:
>
> "Suggestion: Unless you're talking baseball, leave the word "pitch" totally out of your vocabulary. A pitch is something you **do to someone** and **not with good intent**. In sales or whenever you are presenting, you're doing something for someone (or, even with someone) with the best intent; adding value to their lives."

So What Do You *REALLY* Talk About?

You made it through the introduction and small talk; but what will the rest of the conversation focus on?

While your Intriguing Introduction gives you permission to talk about "yourself," you are not actually going to talk all about *you.* If you start to unload your life story, telling them about your accomplishments, your tragedies and how great you are or conversely, complain about your problem or tell a "woe is me" tale, then people will want to move away from you as quickly as they can.

The conversation is in two parts. First, you will briefly explain the topic or theme you set forth in your Intriguing Itroduction. Here are two sample conversations which use two of my Intriguing Introductions:

<u>Sample Conversation #1</u>:

ME: "Hello, I'm Tim Houston and I make businesses and business people more productive, profitable and prosperous."

PERSON: "Really? How do you do that?"

ME: "Well, one of the ways I do that is by helping people and companies to create referral generating systems that produce more qualified referrals, more often. I help my clients by teaching them how to stimulate, motivate, activate and reward the people their networks to give them the qualified referrals that they want, in a predictable, controllable manner."

<u>Sample Conversation #2</u>:

ME: "Most people know that qualified referrals are the ultimate way to generate new business. Yet most people have a hard time getting referred on a regular basis from their clients and contacts. So I help people transform their contacts that count into rich, rewarding referral relationships by helping them to create simple referral generating systems."

PERSON: "What kind of clients do you typically work with?"

ME: "They range from solo-entrepreneurs to international companies. I teach them and in some cases design for them referral systems that are scalable and can be implemented without spending large amounts of time or money and in some cases no money at all."

Focus on Their Favorite Subject

"But enough about me, let's talk about you... what do YOU think of me?"

-- Bette Midler, "Beaches"

After speaking a little bit about yourself, you need to move the conversation onto the second part which features their favorite subject: ***them***.

Dorrie Clark, author of *Stand Out* and an adjunct professor at Duke University's Fuqua School of Business was quoted in *FastCompany* Magazine as saying "It's harder for someone to become bored talking with you when they're talking about themselves." Make sure to keep your own replies brief to allow the other person to give you as much information about themselves as possible. In this way, she believes, you'll be able to focus the discussion on what's most important to them, and create a better bond.[xviii]

The best way to do this is to ask questions that give them permission to talk about themselves. For example, you could ask questions like:

- How long have they been in their field or occupation?
- What made them go into that field?
- What is the most rewarding part of their profession?
- What are the biggest changes to their company or industry over the past 5 years?
- Do they go to any other networking events or belong to any groups? If so, which ones. If not, why not?
- Are there specific people at this event that they would like to be introduced to? (After all, you may know some of the people event and your new friend may have been waiting for someone to make a formal introduction to those people).
- How do they get new clients?
- What would be a good referral for them?
- What can you say/ask/look for that would indicate a person needs their products/service?
- Who/what would be an ideal source of referrals for them?

THE #1 SKILL OF MASTER CONVERSATIONALISTS

The best conversationalists in the world have mastered the skill of listening. Author Simon Sinek says "There is a significant difference between listening and waiting for your turn to speak." He says

> "[L]istening goes far beyond simply paying attention. Becoming a 'good listener' is a skill that requires practice. At this level, listening means trying to find meaning in what you hear. It is not simply about concentrating on what is being said to you; it is the active pursuit of understanding. Good listeners have a huge advantage. For one, when they engage in conversation, they make people 'feel' heard. The people with whom they are speaking 'feel' that someone really understands their wants, needs, and desires. And for good reason; a good listener really does care to understand."[xix]

THE ONE POWERFUL QUESTION THAT IS RARELY ASKED

In each conversation you may want to ask a question that most people – even the most experienced of networkers -- will rarely or never ask at a networking event:

"How can I help you today?"

Don't be surprised if this should cause the other person to stop and think for a moment before they tell you how you can help them. It could be that they want to meet a certain person at the event. Maybe they want certain types of referrals. Perhaps they may invite you to attend an event that they are hosting at a future time.

If they want to meet a certain person and you know that person well enough you may want to facilitate the introduction at the event (assuming you feel comfortable about doing this for your new networking partner). On the other hand, you may want to consider doing it after the event as part of your follow-up sequence.

If they are looking for referrals, ask "What type of referral would be a great referral for you?" Your goal is to get them to elaborate a bit and to teach you specifically who would be the person that you could potentially refer to them in the future. It also sets the stage for a possible future meeting with the person you just met so that you can explore how you may be able to help one another.

TO GIVE OR NOT TO GIVE YOUR BUSINESS CARD

At some point in your conversation with another person or with other people if you're talking a group, you are going to want to be able to give out your business card.

The question most people often ask themselves is **"When is it appropriate to do so?**

There are different rules of business etiquette and customs in various societies and depending where you are in the world, you need to know what those rules and customs are ahead of time.[2]

For example, the way Japanese business people, give, physically handle and use business cards is very different than the way Americans do. In fact, it is a protocol and ritual called *Meishi.* According to Dr. Deborah Swallow, a leading authority on intercultural communication in the U.K.:

---

[2] If you are doing business internationally, I highly recommend that you read Terri Morrison's outstanding book *Kiss, Bow or Shake Hands (The Bestselling Guide to Doing Business in More than 60 Countries).*

"For those in Asian countries, the exchanging of business cards is symbolic; it symbolizes the beginning of a relationship. In Japan, ***meishi koukan*** is so important they even have an etiquette for it. If traveling to that part of the world, ensure that you have a vast amount of cards with you as people formally present cards ***at the beginning of every first meeting***…

"In this part of the world, your business card represents your social status. Unless a business card has been exchanged, no business can take place. If you do not have one, this implies you are of no consequence; you don't exist."[xx]

In the Western World, the very concept of a business card is less formal as it is usually viewed and treated as merely as someone's "contact information." Unlike in Japan, most western people find it rude when upon meeting for the first time someone immediately shoves a business card under their nose. If you give your card upon meeting someone, you assume that the other person wants your contact information. Meanwhile, the other may view it as incredibly intrusive as you are entering their "personal space" without permission.

To avoid this faux pas, there are two simple rules remember:

1. If you are the one who initiated the conversation, do not ask for the other person's business card until *towards the end of the conversation.*
2. Do not give your business card *unless* specifically requested by the other person or if you *ask and receive permission* from them to give your card.

If at any time during the conversation the other person may turn to you and ask for your card, please make sure that your cards are kept in a spot that is easily accessible. Gentlemen, if you are wearing a jacket, make sure you keep your cards in a pocket on one side and use another pocket inside the jacket or perhaps on your shirt to store the cards from the people you have met at the event. Ladies, you may want to keep your cards in a special spot in your purse or carry around a card case so that you aren't fumbling looking for cards to give out.

Nowadays when I attend networking events, many of the younger attendees often would like to receive your contact information but they won't carry their own business cards to offer in return. The "seasoned business" person (i.e. mostly those of us over age 35) may tend to think they are irresponsible or not serious. But please understand that this is a value/judgment call that the younger generation is making from their personal values. (They may want to conserve and save natural resources; they may be living a minimalist lifestyle without the clutter). Whatever their reason, respect it.

Instead of making judgments, offer to compromise:

- Ask them if they have an app like Evernote or CamCard on their smartphone. Offer them your card so that they can take a photo of it as these apps can scan and import your contact information directly into their smartphone's contact manager. (And don't be offended if they give back your card after doing so).

- Then ask them to either text or email you their contact information right there and then, to ensure that you get it.

Whether you receive their business card or contact information, please ask this question:

"I like to keep in touch with the people that I meet. **What is the best way to reach you? Would you like an email, a text or a phone call?"** (This is a very important step for follow-up purposes).

So remember, it is perfectly acceptable to ask for someone's business card or to offer to your own. When you do ask for theirs or offer yours towards the end of the conversation, it not only respects the other people's time and "space" it also makes you a more effective networker.

HOW TO END AND EXIT WITH EASE

"Affairs are easier of entrance than of exit, and it is but common prudence to see our way out before we venture in."

-- Aesop, "The Sick Lion"

Just like an intelligent investor or a skilled military commander, you need to have an exit strategy for knowing when to end a conversation and how to exit the event with ease and while still maintaining your integrity. Yet some people find this to be one of the most awkward parts of networking while others find it rather easy to do.

CONCLUDING THE CONVERSATION

As with all things in life, even the conversation must come to an end. If you are having a hard time ending a conversation, just say to the other person "Thank you for taking the time to speak with me. I wish you all the best!" This helps both you and the other person to remain authentic to one another and leave the conversation gracefully.

If the conversation is a great one but has begun to take up so much time that it will prevent you from networking with and meeting other people, make a plan to continue it at a later time. Say something like: "I'd really love to continue our conversation. Can we set a time to talk or meet later this week?"

Remember, your last impression is just as important as your first impression. As bestselling author Harvey MacKay put it in *Dig Your Well Before You're* Thirsty: "It does matter *how* they remember you, but it is even more important that they *do* remember you."

But what happens when we meet people that won't let us get a word in edge-wise? We feel trapped and while we don't want to be rude, we can't seem to find a way out of the conversation. Diane DiResta, CSP is an author, media trainer, speech coach and certified speech pathologist who teaches us how to verbally apply the brakes to the runaway talker in her blog called "You Talk Too Much: 3 Ways to Get Boring People to Stop Talking". Read it here: **http://www.diresta.com/you-talk-too-much-3-ways-to-get-boring-people-to-stop-talking**

BEWARE THE NETWORKING GHOSTS

You have probably encountered a few ghosts at networking events, mixers, and parties.

No, not the paranormal kind of ghost or the spirit of some deceased business person that's now haunting the venue of the event. I'm talking about a person that you met and may have spent some significant time talking to and socializing with them. At some point, you turn around to interact with them again, and suddenly, just like a ghost...POOF! They're gone!

What happened to them? Did anyone see them leave? Are they just in another room?

Chances are they just left the event without ever saying goodbye to anyone.

The people who do this use a "technique" that now goes by the widely accepted term called "ghosting." (Depending where you are in the world, it may go under a different name with some ethnic connotation i.e. "The Irish Goodbye" "The English/French Exit" "The Dutch Leave" but the "technique" is all the same).

Basically, ghosting means a person exits an event or situation without warning, without saying goodbye and without drawing any attention to themselves. In networking situations, the person who ghosts often has an expectation that most people won't even know that they are gone. So they just disappear. This can happen when meeting someone at a networking event or even afterward as part of the follow-up process.

Although this practice has been around for many decades -- perhaps centuries -- it has become more prevalent among people that are dating who then break up – without warning. Unlike actually saying "this isn't working," people who "ghost" cut off all communication with the other person and to "disappear" from their lives altogether. Some people blame technology and social media for making it easier to ghost and the increasing use of this "break up technique" has caught worldwide media attention from *The New York Times, The Huffington Post, Fox News, The Independent (UK)* and countless blogs -- especially when actress Charlize Theron broke up with actor Sean Penn by ghosting him.

There are some "relationship experts" and media personalities that advocate the practice of ghosting. They argue that instead of feeling awkward when it is time for you to leave a conversation or the event, instead of going around the room saying your goodbyes, they advise people to just leave.

Some like Seth Stevenson, author of *Grounded: A Down to Earth Journey Around the World* advocates the practice of ghosting. In an article on Slate.com called "Don't Say Goodbye. Just Ghost[xxi]" he argues:

> "Still think it's an etiquette breach? Simply replace your awkward goodbye with a heartfelt email sent the following morning. This note can double as a formal thank you to the host—a rare gesture these days, and one that actually does have value."

Why do people ghost? Perhaps they feel anxious or awkward when exiting; perhaps they have a long journey home or really weren't feeling well. Maybe, like Matt Lauer host of *The Today Show* -- a self-confessed ghost – says that "I always slip out…I think that ghosting for people who wake up early is not that rude...We [have] to leave so early from so many of these dinners that if you [just] get up and leave, you put a crimp in the whole dinner.[xxii]"

Jen Kim, a writer for *Psychology Today* had her own encounter with a "ghost" where she was the "victim".

She details her encounter in an article called "The Strange Psychology of Ghosting" and also sought to find the psychological reasoning as to why people would engage in a practice like ghosting. She writes:

"Elliot Aronson, author of *Mistakes Were Made (But Not By Me)* attributes this behavior to *cognitive dissonance*—"a state of tension that occurs whenever a person holds two cognitions [ideas or beliefs] that are psychologically inconsistent." The example he uses is how we know that smoking is bad for our health, yet may continue to smoke several packs per day.

"This dissonance often causes us anguish, which we try to alleviate through self-justification (often rooted in denial). In the smoking example, we might try to quit. If we fail, then we attempt to convince ourselves that we don't really **need** to quit by making up excuses like smoking isn't all that bad, or it helps us lose weight. In other words, **our brains are naturally wired to think that we're right**, even when all the evidence says we're not." [xxiii]

Whatever the reason, the Networking Ghosts use this tactic (I call it bad manners) as it creates a *fait accompli* for the hosts and attendees – people just have to accept that they are gone and there's nothing they can do about it.

Whether you were invited to the event directly by the hosts or as a result of an open invitation and arrived solo or with a friend/colleague, then at the very least, make sure you let them know that you will be leaving ahead of time. This way you don't need to offer an excuse by saying you have to use the bathroom or want to settle your bar tab or have to make a phone call and then duck out of sight or out of the venue.

Excuses and exits like these can and sometimes will come back to haunt those who use them, thanks in large part to social media. It is common to see these ghosts are spotted again, usually elsewhere on the same day. Some Networking Ghosts are photographed or tagged in updates at 7 PM on Facebook but by 8 PM, they are spotted, photographed and tagged on Instagram with another group of people, or are tweeting on Twitter while at another event clear across town When discovered this behavior puts their reputation and credibility in a downward spiral with the very people they met at an earlier event.

A man's manners are a mirror in which he shows his portrait."

-- Johan Wolfgang von Goethe

*Susan RoAne is a highly sought after international speaker and the author of the enduring bestseller, **How to Work A Room** now in its Silver Anniversary Edition. Known internationally as The Mingling Maven®, she offers some practical and powerful advice for those of us who may find it difficult to say goodbye. Learn more about Susan at* **www.susanroane.com** *and follow her on Twitter @susanroane*

ETHICAL ENDINGS AND EXITS BY SUSAN ROANE

How we enter a room, a conversation, a new job, or organization is important and makes a definite impression. How we leave anything – a job, a meeting, a volunteer position, or friendship — speaks volumes about our character. With either action, we can shine or tarnish a professional or personal reputation, but the exit is the final impression. It makes sense to leave the right one.

LITTLE LEAVINGS, ENDLESS ENDINGS

Even life's little endings give some people trouble. They have trouble getting off the phone or leaving a meeting or ending a lunch.

My grandmother perfected her phone call endings. When she was ready to hang up, she would sweetly say, "Thank you so much for calling," and before you could respond, you heard the phone click.

Experts recommend that we wait until we're talking, then interrupt ourselves to say, "Glad we had a chance to speak about the issue. Hope all goes well. Goodbye."

Yes, that does invest the time it takes to say 14 words for what could be, "Gotta go," but it's a good investment and a smart one that shows manners, consideration, and maturity.

Then there are those who must control the conversation; whether it's business conversation or a personal one and be the first to say goodbye. One person told of an acquaintance who consistently calls the end to conversations, but if she should excuse herself and say goodbye first, he holds her with a "just more thing," rehashing what has been said or making another comment until *he* can end the conversation.

Yes, Conversation Control Freaks do exist, but we can handle them. Should they jump over our goodbye with a comment, politely say "I really must go" and, like Grandma, "hang up" on them and move on.

LET MY PEOPLE GO!

As a guest, it's important to know when and how to leave a party so we don't overstay our welcome. As the host, when someone says their goodbyes we need to let them go.

Whether it's on the phone, at an event, or at a meeting, we need to hear the hint and take it. This isn't the moment to monopolize a person's time. Look for another person standing alone or visit the buffet dessert table. There will always be people having fun with fattening foods and chocolate.

When leaving any event, the best exit is the mandatory, verbal "thank you" to the host, appropriate good-byes to those guests who merit a cheery goodbye, and then… leave! A lengthy goodbye can be very irritating to the spouses, friends, or co-workers who are waiting around for us to leave with them, wondering what is taking so long.

Being prepared to exit face to face conversations, gatherings or jobs with grace, and manners make the Right Impression.

> *"Every exit is an entry to somewhere else."*
>
> *-- Tom Stoppard*

CHAPTER 3:

AFTER NETWORKING KNOW-HOWS

The Fortune is in The Follow-Through And The Follow-Up

"It was character that got us out of bed, commitment that moved us into action and discipline that enabled us to follow through."

– Zig Ziglar

While it is great to make new contacts, it is not the culmination of the networking experience. The event may have ended, but the most important phase of the relationship building process has just begun. You now need to begin a series of engagements with the people you just met in order to transform them from just being contacts into meaningful connections.

For all that has been written and talked about the importance of following up on a promise or commitment, many people continuously do not. Psychologists, academics, and other experts speculate that people fail to do so for a variety of reasons: they don't have or make the time to do so; they may be fearful, they expect the other person to follow-up first, they forget, they become overwhelmed, etc. (You can insert your own reason or excuse here).

In my book *The Referral Rules*, Rule #6 is called "Follow-Up or Fall Out." In that chapter, I cited three separate studies that examined the failure of sales people in following up with qualified sales leads and prospects. Each of these studies concluded that as many as 55% to 85% of salespeople failed to follow-up with the very people who had expressed an interest in a product or service. From my perspective, the worst part is that the prospects *gave their permission* to the salesperson **to follow up and contact them**![3]

My experience is that people ultimately fail because although they have the best of intentions to follow-up, they lack an efficient follow-up system and the discipline to follow-through on their follow-ups. Instead of keeping things simple, they over-complicate the process (either in their mind or in reality — sometimes both) or become

---

[3] While *The Referral Rules* details 7 ways to get more qualified, profitable referrals, in order to get to that level, you need to first follow up with the people you meet while networking in order to start to build a relationship with them.

distracted to the point where they become stuck. Thus nothing happens and the networking time spent with them was wasted.

To help me keep me focused on following through in following up with new contacts, I created the following system.

TIM'S 3-STEP FOLLOW-THROUGH SYSTEM

1. After initially meeting and conversing with someone, it may become apparent that you would like to follow-up with them. Towards the end of the conversation, let your expectation be known and give a reason why you would like to follow-up with them. If they agree to further communication, prepare them for the next contact by a) asking them what is their preferred method of communication? (Email, Text, phone call?) and b) let them know that you will be contacting them within 24-48 hours just to recap your initial meeting and to schedule a more detailed follow-up call/meeting/interaction. That way when the initial conversation is over, the expectation for further communication is set with both parties.

2. Assuming the person doesn't say "let's schedule it" right then and there, when you exit the conversation, open up your calendar on your smartphone (or pull out your

paper calendar) and schedule the follow-up and indicate the preferred method. (ex. "Initial follow-up with James Smith from Acme Industries via text). Set a reminder 30 minutes beforehand so that you have time to review your notes and prepare for the next interaction. (Refer to chapter 2 and to the next section in this chapter for additional prep points).

3. Then do it! You told the people you met that you would follow-up with them and you did. Considering most people won't follow-through on following-up, not only does this makes you stand out, it plants the seeds of comfort in their minds that should they choose to build a relationship with you and eventually refer someone to you. They will think and expect that you will truly "walk the talk" because you took the time and had the initiative to follow-through.

HOW ABOUT NOW?

Patti DiNucci, author of *The Intentional Networker* suggests trying an immediate follow-through technique:

> "Let's say you just met someone at a networking event and they are interested in getting to know you better. If your schedule allows (and you can be proactive in setting aside the time), suggest that you meet for ten to fifteen minutes right after the event you are currently attending. Stay true to the time limit. After investing this relatively small amount of time with this person, you may be able to gauge whether or not a longer one-on-one date in order down the road." [xxiv]

FLAWLESS FOLLOW-UP IN 4 STEPS

The manner in which you follow-up is also important. Here is a very simple system that I use to make my immediate follow-up efforts easy:

1. When I finish a conversation with someone, I write a quick note about them on the back of their business card containing where I met them, what we discussed and maybe something I learned about them in the conversation. **I then take a photograph of**

the front and back of the card just in case it gets misplaced. After the event, I use the app Evernote to keep these photographs and notes organized and I also transcribe my handwritten notes from the back of the card into Evernote.

2. The time in which you follow up with people that you have met speaks volumes about you as a person as well as the business you represent. I, like most experts, believe that following up within 24-48 hours of meeting someone is ideal because it shows that you have integrity. I send what I call an Extraordinary Email to the people I met. This goes beyond just saying "it was a pleasure meeting you." In each email, I try to be of value to the recipient by focusing on a need of theirs or a subject that came up in our conversation. I also try to provide them with useful information that would be of help or assistance to them. While I will never ask them for anything in return, the Law of Reciprocity is put into effect and

they will likely respond and perhaps will offer to help me. This sets the stage for further dialogue. You can see a sample of an extraordinary email by going to **nononsensenetworking.com/resources**

3. In addition to the email, I will also send them a card or quick hand-written a note. The power of a handwritten note has been proven over the ages to work very well. If your handwriting is like mine (i.e. less than perfect) or if you just want a fast, simple way to send a real, personalized greeting card via first-class mail to someone in less than a minute, I highly recommend using Sendoutcards.com.

4. Assuming the other person has not reached out to connect with me on social media first, I will usually send a request to connect with them on LinkedIn or Facebook or follow them on Twitter *after* they have responded to my initial follow-up email or note. This way it is less intrusive because we have a

dialogue taking place. When I do connect with or follow them on social media, I never try to sell to them. What does happen though is that this connection helps to keep us in front of one another as we will likely see each other's posts.

THE ONE THING...

There's one thing that most people never do that causes them to miss out on some amazing relationship building opportunities. This one thing can make you very memorable if you do it consistently. It can also set the stage for very high-value referrals in a faster way, from a variety of sources.

The one thing is when you engage the hosts/organizers of a networking event.

Follow these steps and you will definitely stand out and will likely be contacted:

1. Contact the host/organizer post-event to ask if an attendee list can be made available for follow-up purposes. (Please note you're not going to use this list to SPAM everyone but you will use the information for another purpose as discussed in this chapter).

2. Send an email/note to the organizers thanking them for having such a great event and ask them to keep you

informed of any upcoming or additional events that they will be hosting.

3. In your note or email, offer to volunteer or help out at their an upcoming event. Ask them what would be the best way for you to serve their needs.

4. Offer to promote their future events to those you know who may be interested. Share links to their website on social media, promoting it in emails and by telling others who may be interested.

5. Offer a written testimonial that they can use in promotional materials and on social media.

HOW TO MEET PEOPLE YOU DIDN'T MEET

There may be people at a networking event that you wanted to meet but didn't have the opportunity to do so. If you have obtained a list of the attendees, scan the list and pick out three to five people who you would like to connect with. Better yet, if one of your colleagues or friends knows one of the people who you missed meeting and ask them for an introduction.

If you haven't already done so, do some Online Observations or Social Media Surveillance on these people, taking note of something that would be of authentic, rapport-building value between you and them, both on a personal and professional level.

For example, you may discover that a person posted that they did a certain type of charity work or their LinkedIn profile indicates that they have experience with clients in a market or industry that you deal with. You may have seen pictures on Facebook or Instagram of their Mediterranean cruise of the Greek Isles. Maybe they speak a second or third language that you speak or are learning. Maybe you both went to the same college or have a certain connection or friend in common.

Once you identified one or two rapport points, send them a short, straight-to-the-point email or a note stating the reason why you are contacting them. For example:

Dear Mr. Johnson,

I'm sorry I didn't get a chance to meet you at the Tri-City Business Expo this week. I am reaching as requesting that we could speak for a few minutes as I would like to learn more about your company's new marketing service that is geared towards the dry cleaning industry which I read about it on your company's website. Since I have been working very closely with many dry cleaners across the state for the past four years, it looks like a program that I may be able to promote to my existing clients and ultimately refer them to you.

If you are interested, would you please be so kind as to email me a few dates and times that you are available to speak this week?   My email is jdellwood@mycompany.com.

Best Regards,

Jennifer Dellwood.

If they don't reply, just follow up once with them. If they don't reply to that final follow-up, move on. Don't stalk, beg, or berate them as they may not be interested at this point in time. Keep in touch with them by giving something of value to them, such as information or resources which could help them or their clients.

If they do reply, schedule the call and respect their time. Let them talk, listen and ask questions of them. Do not try to sell your services or products to them as you are still engaging them. Your next step is to try to arrange a face-to-face meeting where you will have an opportunity to be with them and determine if you can be of service to them and them to you.

YOUR NEXT STEPS

---

*The great aim of education is
not knowledge but action.*

-- Herbert Spencer

Your networking is not going to work until you take action.

No matter what type of events you attend, you have the opportunity to meet people that you wouldn't ordinarily meet in the course of a year – perhaps a lifetime. Over time and with mastering the skills and techniques that are in *No-Nonsense Networking,* some of these very people will become life-long business partners, referral sources, and friends.

As you embark on taking the next steps to transforming your contacts into connections that count, remember to add as much value as you can to their lives and to their business. The more you give, the more you will receive back from the people in your networks.

So get out there and network! There's a world of people waiting to meet you and for you to be of service to.

BEFORE YOU GO…

I want to thank you for spending time reading *No-Nonsense Networking*. If you found the book to be enjoyable, useful, educational or helpful in any way, I would be very grateful if you would post a short review on Amazon.com or wherever you purchased a copy of this book.

I believe that anyone who is a teacher is also an eternal student as well. Your support and feedback is greatly appreciated and helps me to continuously improve in order to deliver a quality experience for you, the reader.

I do read all of the reviews and comments personally and promise to make future editions of this book and future projects even better.

To leave a review, all you need to do is follow this link to the book's page on your country's Amazon site: **http://geni.us/HeiLBr**

MEET TIM HOUSTON

The super-simple bio: He's a father, a #1 Bestselling Author, an in-demand Speaker, high-energy and motivational Trainer and an Entrepreneur with more than 20 years of making businesses & people more productive, profitable and prosperous.

The professional bio: Timothy M. Houston is an entrepreneur who has started, owned and/or managed four businesses during the past 20 years. Still being a small business owner, his advice and authority are from continuous, daily experience "in the trenches — not from the ivory tower."

He the author of three #1, international bestselling books: (*The World's Worst Networker, Leads to Referrals* and *The Referral Rules!)* and a contributor to the New York Times, and #1 Wall Street Journal and USA Today bestseller, *Masters of Sales*.

Whether as an in-demand keynote speaker, a high-energy trainer or through his online programs, he has worked with business people in more than 60 countries to become more productive, profitable and prosperous.

IN HIS OWN WORDS: "I like to think of myself as a guy who, after 20+ years of real-life business experience, often offers unique and sometimes common-sense approaches to solving what seems like complex problems for businesspeople.

I have been very fortunate to work with people from around the world who come from all walks of life and are at different levels of success. I love teaching them how to make their networking and referral marketing and generation efforts to be more productive, profitable and prosperous."

To learn how I may be able to help you, visit **www.tmhouston.com** and follow me on Twitter **@tmhouston**

DOWNLOAD YOUR FREE COPY!

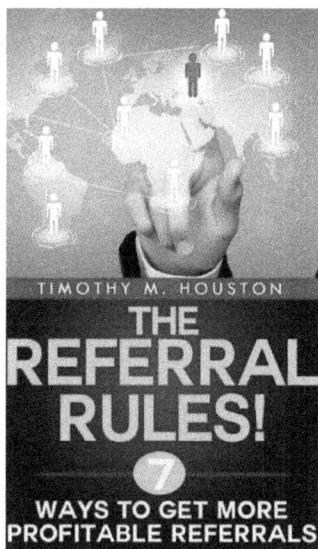

EXCLUSIVE

FREE DOWNLOAD

Get your FREE Ebook Copy of The Referral Rules when you sign up for Tim Houston's VIP Mailing List.

In just 1 hour or less learn how you can use 7 time-tested, basic and proven methods to get others to generate more, higher quality and higher paying referrals for your business.

Get Started here:

www.tmhouston.com/trr

Endnotes

---

[i] Source: http://www.bni.com/Default.aspx?tabid=721 Accessed August 3, 2015

[ii] Source http://dictionary.reference.com/browse/reason?s=t. Accessed August 3, 2015

[iii] Source: http://dictionary.reference.com/browse/goal?s=t Accessed August 3, 2015

[iv] Bergman, K., Friederike, E. and Kopp, S. "A Second Chance to Make a First Impression? How Appearance and Nonverbal Behavior Affect Perceived Warmth and Competence of Virtual Agents Over Time." Conference paper. *Intelligence Virtual Agents 12th Annual Conference, 2012, Santa Cruise, USA.* Retrieved from https://www.researchgate.net/publication/230556524 (Accessed November 7, 2015)

[v] Peplau, L., Taylor, S., Sears, D.: *Social Psychology.* Prentice Hall (2005)

[vi] Source: https://en.wikipedia.org/wiki/Wingman_%28social%29

[vii] May, Cindi, (3rd December 2013) "The Cheerleader Effect." Retreived from http://www.scientificamerican.com/article/the-cheerleader-effect (Accessed June 21, 2016)
[viii] Barth, F. Diane, (24 April 2015), "5 Ways to Make Small Talk Worth the Trouble". Retrieved from https://www.psychologytoday.com/blog/the-couch/201504/5-ways-make-small-talk-worth-the-trouble (Accessed August 11, 2015)

[ix] RoAne, Susan. What Do I Say Next? Talking Your Way to Business and Social Success. 9: Warner Books, 1997. Print

[x] Shah, Shikha, (23 December 2014) "Why Small Talk is a Big

Deal". Retrieved from http://timesofindia.indiatimes.com/life-style/relationships/work/Why-small-talk-is-a-big-deal/articleshow/22888857.cms (Accessed August 11, 2015)

[xi] Misner, Ivan "Why Everyone Should Talk About Politics While Networking", *Entrepreneur,* August 9, 2012. Retrieved from https://www.entrepreneur.com/article/224156 (Accessed 30th May, 2016)

[xii] Chapmin, John J., *The Sales Encyclopedia. The Most Comprehensive "How To" Guide on Selling.* Chapter 23, "Interacting with the Competition". 2009 Eagle View Publishing Ebook. Available at Amazon.com

[xiii] Gallup, Honesty/Ethics in Professions, (December 8-11, 2014). Retrieved from http://www.gallup.com/poll/1654/honesty-ethics-professions.aspx. (Accessed August 11, 2015)

[xiv] Fottrell, Quentin, (11 August 2015) "Here is the pay raise you can expect next year..." Retrieved from http://www.marketwatch.com/story/here-is-the-pay-raise-you-can-expect-next-year-2015-08-11

[xv] Sanburn, Josh (27 June 2013) "You Probably Hate Your Job – But You Don't Have To". Retrieved from http://business.time.com/2013/06/27/you-probably-hate-your-job-but-you-dont-have-to (Accessed August 11, 2014)

[xvi] Soergel, Andrew (30 March 2015), "Almost Half of Americans Aren't Saving Nearly Enough." Retrieved from http://www.usnews.com/news/articles/2015/03/30/almost-half-of-americans-arent-saving-nearly-enough. (Accessed 12 August 2015)

[xvii] Soergel, Andrew (23 February 2015) "1 in 3 Americans Near Financial Disaster". Retrieved from http://www.usnews.com/news/blogs/data-mine/2015/02/23/study-suggests-1-in-3-americans-flirting-with-financial-disaster

xviii Dishman, Lydia. "What to Say at Networking Events to Eliminate Awkward Moments" *Fast Company* October 2015. Retrieved from http://www.fastcompany.com/3052732/how-to-be-a-success-at-everything/how-to-figure-out-what-to-say-at-networking-events (Accessed 7 November 2015)

xix Sinek, Simon, "How to Listen" Retrieved from http://blog.startwithwhy.com/refocus/2010/06/there-is-a-difference-between-listening-and-waiting-for-your-turn-to---speak-just-because-someone-can-hear-doesnt-mean-t.html (Accessed 1 June 2016)

xx Swallow, Deborah. "Everthing You Need to Know About Business Card Meishi Etiquette". Retrieved from http://www.deborahswallow.com/2009/08/22/japan-everything-you-need-to-know-about-business-card-meishi-etiquette/ (Accessed 21 June, 2016)

xxi Stevenson, Seth, "Don't Say Goodbye, Just Ghost." Retrieved from http://www.slate.com/articles/life/a_fine_whine/2013/07/ghosting_the_irish_goodbye_the_french_leave_stop_saying_goodbye_at_parties.html (Accessed 25 October 2015)

xxii The Today Show, October 2, 2014. Retrieved from http://www.hulu.com/watch/703463 (Accessed 25 October, 2015)

xxiii Kim, Jen (2015, July 15th) "The Strange Psychology of Ghosting." Retrieved from: https://www.psychologytoday.com/blog/valley-girl-brain/201507/the-strange-psychology-ghosting (Accessed 15 May, 2016)

xxiv DiNucci, Patti The Intentional Networker: Attracting Powerful Relationships, Referrals and Results in Business. 2011, Rosewall Press. Ebook Available at Amazon.com